My Friend Kate is a Forest Ranger

By Betty Fulcomer

PublishAmerica
Baltimore

© 2010 by Betty Fulcomer.
All rights reserved. No part of this book may be reproduced, stored in a retrieval system or transmitted in any form or by any means without the prior written permission of the publishers, except by a reviewer who may quote brief passages in a review to be printed in a newspaper, magazine or journal.

First printing

ISBN: 978-1-4560-1485-8
PUBLISHED BY PUBLISHAMERICA, LLLP
www.publishamerica.com
Baltimore

Printed in the United States of America

Lightning strikes started three fires yesterday afternoon in the Apache-Sitgreaves National forest in north central Arizona.

"How were the fires seen and reported?" "How are the fires put out?"

"Will some fires be allowed to burn?" I asked my friend Kate a million questions.

"These are all important questions," Kate says. "Come with me and I'll show you the answers."

My friend Kate Klein is a District Ranger, or forester at the Heber Ranger Station in Heber, Arizona, She oversees the western portion of the Apache-Sitgreaves National Forest.

Kate drives the Forest Service green truck from the Heber Ranger Station to the Deer Springs Lookout.

"Can you climb this?" Kate asks.

"Don't look down while you're climbing," she suggests.

At the top of the tower, Kate enters a little room through a trap door. Joyce Williams, the tower observer, holds the door as Kate and I step through.

The view from the top of this lookout is worth the climb. Joyce explains that this 125 foot tower built in 1917 was the first in this forest.

It's my first time in a lookout tower and in the distance I think I see smoke! "That's not smoke," Joyce tells us.

"When it's a rainy day here in the mountains, rain often falls from the clouds and doesn't reach the earth. It's called verga."

"What do you do when you think you see a real fire?" I ask Joyce.

"If I did see smoke, I would use my radio to call another tower observer. She, or he would call a third tower. Each of us would use our triangulators to sight the fire and locate it on a map. Our three sightings from different points would give an exact location. That's called triangulation.

Joyce draws a picture of what she means. "Yesterday, lightning strikes started three fires. The Gentry tower spotted the first one and called me. "Can you see it, too?" they ask.

"I called Juniper Ridge Tower to confirm my spot."

"Rain put out two of the fires. A fire crew was called to put out the third one. Two of the guys are cleaning up below," said Joyce.

Just then, a flash of lightning caught my attention. "Lightning? Do you stay up here in a lightning storm?"

"Sure," Joyce chuckled. "If it gets close, I stand on my stool."

Joyce wasn't kidding! She made sure I noticed the old style glass electrical insulators she had placed on the bottom of the little step stool.

Beneath the tower, Mark and Matt are cleaning their equipment after last night's fire fighting. Their clothes appear wet and dirty. Matt inspects the hose before he winds it up.

"The ground was real hot last night," Mark tells me. "It's a good thing we wear fire retardant clothing and thick-soled boots." "I'm wearing the same kind," Kate tells him.

With pride, Mark shares the details of last night's fire with Kate.

"Lucky for us, it rained last night. That helped us to put the fire out."

"Weather conditions can help us or hurt us when we fight a fire," he said.

Mark and Matt are part of a fire containment team that is assigned an area of 50 square miles in the Heber District of the Apache-Sitgreaves National Forest. Each Ranger District is divided into fire containment response areas. Our Fire Management Office has five engines, a crew for each, and a bulldozer. We also have a hot shot crew. A hot shot crew is a ground crew that goes where vehicles can't go. When there is a fire emergency in another area, the hot shot crew can go anywhere in the southwest to assist.

Our drive back to Kate's office takes us through a forest of Ponderosa pine and Gamble Oak.

"Do you want to see what a fire does to the forest?" Kate asks.

"People camping near here thought that their campfire was out, but it wasn't.

This blackened Ponderosa will probably recover, but the plants growing on the forest floor are not as lucky." Kate's thick-soled boots keep her feet from feeling the heat that's left over from yesterday's fire.

"We have learned a lot about forest growth from studying the effects of fires. Kate picks up a burned branch. "A firefighter can look up into the trees and see the direction that the needles are pointing.

That tells him where the fire is moving. Grass, on the other hand, will fall back from where the fire came from. These two indicators help to give the firefighter more safety in the field."

"Our weather station gives the firefighters advanced warning that fire conditions are present. After lunch, I'll show you that, too."

Kate shows me a good effect of fire in the forest.

"It seems that Ponderosa pine cones open and germinate more quickly when they are heated. This fire will mark a new growth period for this area."

"Eleven years ago, a lost camper started a fire to attract attention. This caused a major fire that burned 1,000 acres and killed five people. The fire burned so hot and so long that the soil became sterilized. Two years after the fire, the Forest Service seeded the area with the same kinds of plants that had been growing there. This is one way we can prevent erosion after a fire."

"This little oak seems to be doing nicely."

Whenever Kate plans to be out of her office and in the forest, she tries to take advantage of her lunchtime opportunities. I'm not surprised when we drive into a meadow with cows enjoying their lunch.

"This is one of my favorite places for lunch," she says. Kate crosses her ankles and sits right down in a shady spot under a large cottonwood tree. The cows look at us as we would look at other diners in any restaurant.

Kate knows that nearby some University of Arizona archeologists are exploring a prehistoric settlement.

"Can you climb a bit?" she asks.

The hillside is rocky and heavily wooded. Kate looks like she feels at home in the forest. She's wearing heavy leather lace-up work boots, yet she zig-zags easily up the hill. She's at the top waiting for me and she's not breathing hard. She smiles as I puff up the hill.

"There's a good view to the west," she says as she beckons me to the other side.

At the top, it's easy to imagine that this hill would have been a safe and easy place to defend for ancient people. The only way up is from the side we climbed.

The view below is excellent. As we head back to the truck, Kate explains how the Forest Service conserves the forest for all of us.

"The forest here serves many purposes. The job of the Forest Service is to balance the uses and to make sure that the forest does not suffer from this use."

"Major users are timber industries, public and private, recreation, grazing, watershed management, and wildlife protection. I'll show you how these are interrelated."

Kate takes me to an area where Youth Conservation Corp workers are building the fence to separate a cattle grazing area from a tree growth control area. The fence will keep both cattle and elk from grazing along the wash. This will allow cottonwood trees and other plants to grow and stabilize the banks of the wash to provide erosion control.

When the cattle were allowed to roam freely, they would walk along the bank of the wash looking for new cottonwood shoots. The cottonwood trees are important for wildlife as well as for stabilization of the soil along the wash.

Other Youth Conservation Corp workers are repairing a well so the cattle can have drinking water.

Ranchers pay to let their cattle graze on National Forest land. In Arizona, a rancher with 100 head of cattle would need to have at least 20,000 acres for them to feed for one year.

But by paying to graze on National Forest land, the rancher can move his cattle from one grazing area to another as he gives his land a chance to re-grow the grass that the cattle have eaten.

Each year, Kate's office must read requests for grazing and develop a new operating plan. One sheep and 12 cattle permits are authorized for the Heber Ranger District. A permit is issued for 10 years.

Kate shows me that Blue Gramma Grass, a warm season grass, is growing here. The cows like Blue Gramma but will often choose other less common, more tasty varieties first. If livestock use is not controlled, it can greatly reduce the variety of grasses growing on the rangelands.

To insure that the other kinds of grass have an opportunity to grow back, cows will not be allowed to graze here at the same time next year. To make sure this rule is followed, the Forest Service will install a photo point to monitor the number of cows and the season when they are grazing.

Kate returns to her office at the Heber Ranger Station.

Kate visits Loretta Kelly in the Geographic Information System room. To analyze last night's fire containment, Loretta is using two computer systems. One plots the fire size, location, and rate of spread on a map. The other computer program predicts fire behavior based on wind speed, relative humidity, and temperature.

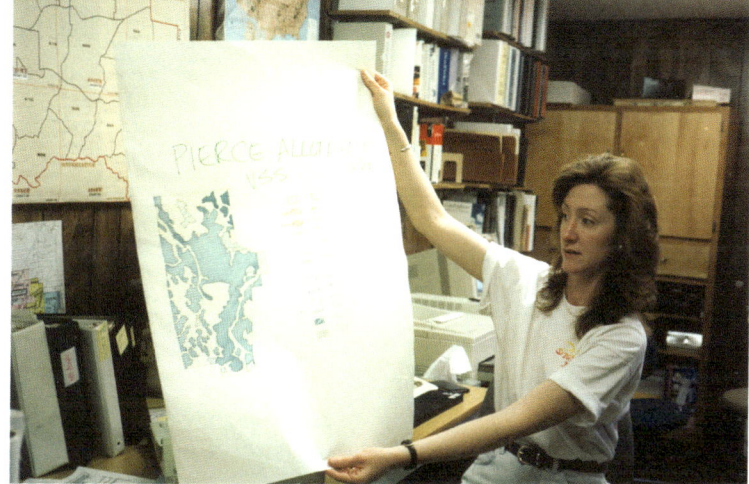

Loretta links the fire behavior information with a fire history occurrence for the area and prints a map for Kate. Since the first fire was spotted, all of the crews have communicated with the fire management officer and Kate.

"How do you get weather service data so reliable for this area?" I ask. We walk to a large fenced area behind the Ranger Station. "This is the Heber, Arizona reporting station," Kate explains.

"This is the solar powered rain gauge that measures snow depth. It will help us to predict the spring rain and snow run-off which affects roads dams, streams, as well as cattle grazing."

In the weather station, Kate notices that the relative humidity is rising.

"Will it rain later?" I ask hopefully.

Amounts of rain, snow, humidity, temperature and types of clouds are all reported to the National Weather Service.

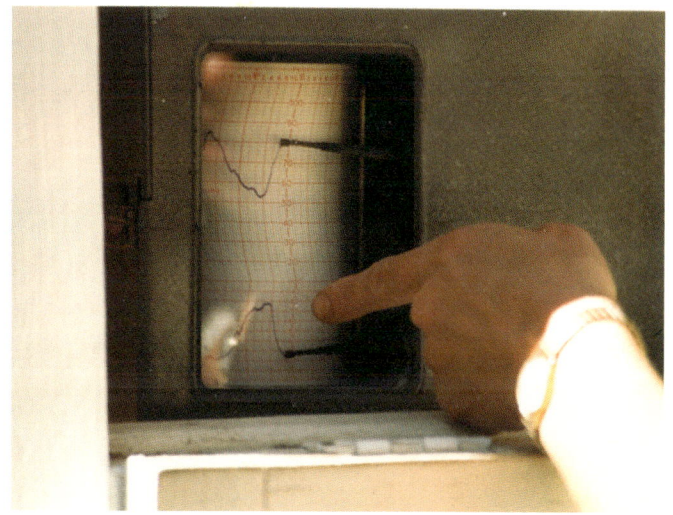

I see what looks like a musical instrument made of sticks tied to the fence. "These are fuel sticks," Kate explains.

"They measure the amount of moisture when they are compared to a computer model.

"You may want to talk to a Fire Safety Expert about how they are used."

"Wind direction and wind speed affect the way a fire can be put out. Keeping accurate weather records gives us a better chance in the next fire," Kate says.

"During a going fire, temperature, humidity and fuel moisture levels can help us to understand the fire's behavior. A fire can actually create its own weather."

In a large complex behind the Ranger Station office, Kate takes me to the equipment barn. I see water carrier trucks, firefighter crew trucks, pumper engines. Behind the vehicles are small shops for repairs.

A hot shot crew has just returned from fighting a fire in a forest nearly 100 miles away. Kate talks with the workers who maintain the engines and fire equipment.

We stop to speak to a group of firefighters who are cleaning their six hundred gallon water tank and testing their hose. This one has a leak! Since it must carry 250 pounds of pressure, this hose will be retired and used only for cleaning up.

If the hose had not been damaged, it would have been drained and dried on this drying rack.

Near the equipment area these workers have been practicing loading and unloading horses from the trailer. Horses are often used to survey sensitive areas where motorized vehicles are not allowed. These men have already passed their riding test. Many of the employees in this area need to know how to ride on horseback.

Physical training is an important aspect of firefighting. Firefighting is exciting and physically demanding work that requires endurance more than just brute strength. To help keep the crews fit, a training course with exercise stations is beside the equipment area.

"Women can do this work. What a great summer experience this would be for a female college student who wanted to work hard, learn a lot and have a physically fit summer. There are many opportunities for women beyond the seasonal work."

"How did you get into the Forest Service?" I asked.

"I went to Ursinus College, then Penn State in Pennsylvania where I was in a Pre-Med program. The more I studied biology, the more I liked it. But when I took a course in forestry, that was it! I loved being in the woods."

"After college, I joined the Peace Corp. I lived in Honduras for two years. A teacher I had in second grade left to join the Peace Corp. Maybe that idea was in my mind for a long time."

"I have always loved the woods. My sister, three brothers and I spent great summers on our grandparents' farm in Missouri. We fished and played in the fields."

"I was really into sports. I played field hockey, lacrosse, tennis, and basketball. Sports helped me to learn that it takes much effort and persistence to succeed. I knew that whatever job I would go for needed to be challenging. I knew that I wanted a job that would make me apply responsibility, creativity, persistence and a challenge- either physical, mental or both, for me to choose it for my career."

"This job involves all of that, and more. I'm a wife and mother, too."

Later in the day, Kate told me her "persistence" story.

For weeks, all her friends talked about was how they were training for a city bicycle race in Philadelphia. Finally, she agreed to go along.

Wearing cut-off jeans and a tee shirt, she felt out of place with riders wearing racing style gear all around her. Her bike was an old ten-speed Schwinn.

The race was a 24 hour marathon. You could stop for water and meals, but the idea was to clock as many miles as possible.

One by one, all of her friends dropped out of the race. After a whole day and night, she had ridden 265 miles through the streets of downtown Philadelphia. She came in second in the women's division and won a bicycle!

This race and other sports experiences have helped Kate to know that when all seems too tough, or too hard, or too trying, she shouldn't give up. She thinks that sports helped her to know about persistence.

Sports training also helps her to have endurance.

I ask Kate about wood cutting in the National Forest.

"Perhaps the best reason there is a National Forest Service is to serve as a balance between use and resource. Many of the people in the community make their living from the forest. By protecting the forest, we hope to insure their livelihood for years to come."

"Before the National Forest Service, sawmills were set up along streams. In many cases, the stream would carry the cut trees downstream to the mill. Workers would cut areas close to the mill first, then moving in bigger and bigger circles, they would clear cut great parts of the forest."

"The first saw mills in the Arizona forest area were owned by people from the East Coast like North Carolina who had cut all of the available forest there, then moved into Arizona to supply timber for the great growth of California and the West."

"Nowadays, we think we're doing a better job of forest management. We use the GIS computer system to section the forest into plots. This is my absolute favorite part. We go into the forest, and count the number of trees, noting the type, the size, height, and diameter of each."

"Before any trees are cut, a forester will do a forest inventory, or tree age measurement. When the height of the trees is known, a table lists them on a site index curve. Then using a computer model, the speed of the trees' growth is plotted. Only then can the timber volume of the forest be anticipated.

"How well will the trees that are left grow after the cutting? That must be our first consideration when we choose to cut in forest" the Kate tells me.

"When we find an old tree like this one, we will use this boring tool to take a core sample. We compare the space between rings when the tree was young, to the spaces in its more recent growth. We also check for CWD, that's coarse woody debris, important for habitats but perhaps a danger for forest fire behavior.

I ask Kate more questions. "With the amount of rainfall received in a particular plot, how many trees can live? Are too many pine trees choking out the native oak? Are dense stands of trees with many hanging snags creating fuel loading problems around housing developments?"

"To confirm the age of the trees after cutting, we count tree rings. Each ring stands for one year of growth."

"If we see that the tree rings are evenly spaced, then the rainfall has been uniform. But if the rings are tightly packed so we can hardly count them, then that plot may not be getting enough rainfall to keep the younger trees growing. Sometimes trees will be cut to slow water use in an area."

"In most cases, we'll use a computer model based on the type of soil, amount of rainfall and kind of tree to determine how to allow for cutting.

The Forest Service will always do an environmental study with particular attention to wildlife and the Forest Service will provide a prescription for health. Then, only the Forest Service will mark the trees to be cut."

"In years past, we believed in overstory removal which says that all trees with a diameter of more than 9 inches should be cut. That will allow younger trees to have enough sunlight to grow.

But comparative studies found that the edge of the forest was most productive in terms of tree growth and wildlife diversity. Birds may nest in tall trees, but they'll do most of their hunting and food gathering on the forest's edge. That's where their "dinner" is also looking for food."

"By looking at the whole range, we try for small, medium, and large trees living together. That's called uneven age management. This is the presently adopted goal of the National Forest Service."

As we are taking turns using the boring tool, another Forest Service green truck stops by Kate's.

It's Don, the forester in charge of the forest inventory.

Just down the road, men with sprayers are painting yellow or orange marks on trees to mark them not to be cut during the next pulpwood cutting.

Trees bigger than 16 inches in diameter are not cut. Trees to be saved from cutting must be sprayed on two places on each tree, once at near-ground level, the other about 6 to 10 feet up so the mark is very visible to the tree cutter who will be wearing protective goggles which impair his vision.

Don tells Kate that he's not seeing the yellow marks in perfect placement and he asks Kate to come by to see what he means.

We follow Don to where Brent and Ben are spray marking yellow or orange. It's easy to recognize the painters! Their clothes are decorated with splatters of yellow and orange.

Ben is especially proud of his shoes. He claims that he's the "fashion guy."

Kate talks with them about why some of the marks need to be made differently. Everyone seems comfortable talking about how and why the changes are necessary.

Many people who work for the National Forest Service are seasonal or temporary workers. During the summer, this ranger station employs 90 people. This includes teacher project directors, fire crew members, campground facilitators and tree markers like Ben and Brett.

Many trees in this forest show blue marks. Kate explains that blue means that these trees have been selected to be cut and only Forest Service personnel make the marks. Again, we see the mark at the bottom of the tree as well as 6 feet to 10 feet up.

Only the Forest Service is allowed to mark the trees to be cut for either commercial or non-commercial use. Commercial cutters need to apply for a permit, usually bidding against other cutters.

Trees cut from this forest provide building material for homes and industry. Small or irregular trees that may have been rejected for wood cutting some years ago are workable using new saw mill methods. Even wood scraps are useful. With glue added to wood pulp and scraps, pressboard and particle board products are often stronger than board lumber. Cardboard, packing material and other paper products are all manufactured near here.

Also, people who live here can get a permit to cut firewood to heat their homes. These permits are free or very low cost.

Kate has spent the day showing me the forest she loves. The fires that started with lightning have been put out.

No one working here was injured today.

The people who work with Kate appreciate the forest as a great resource and the responsibility they owe to it.

If every day could be like today, Kate would be pleased.

Glossary

boring tool - A tool that takes a sample of the core of a tree to remove a cylinder of wood containing a cross-section of the tree's growth rings

containment - The fire management team decides that the fire and danger of flare-ups is over because a fuel break around the fire has been completed.

fuel stick - sticks which help to compare the moisture content of different kinds of wood samples from air temperature, humidity, insolation and rainfall.

grazing - allowing cows or other range animals to eat naturally growing foliage

insolation - exposure to the sun's rays

insulators - telephone glass pieces that prevent electrical current

overstory removal - trees of a forest of more than one story that forms the upper canopy layer. A horizontal layer in a plant community

persistence - not giving up when a job is hard

slash- branches, treetops, bark and other debris following a harvest

sterilized- burned so hot that nothing on the forest floor will grow

timber- trees grown and tended for regulated crops for cutting timber volume

triangulator- a device that creates a line of sight for finding a fixed point on a map

triangulation- three sightings from different points used to give an exact location

watershed management- an area of land that receives water as rain or snow and discharges it into a single stream or other outlet

uniform- regular spaces between tree rings

uneven age management- a process through select cutting and thinning to cause multiple ages of desireable trees in an area. A group of trees of a variety of ages and sizes and often different species

verga- rain that does not reach the ground

Sources used for Glossary:

Fire Behavior SDK 1.0.0 http//fire.org/downloads/fbsdk/docs/html/pages.html

http://www.morcd.org/totorcd/Forestry%20Terms.htm Doug Enyart

Timberline Forestry Consulting LLCGeoff Kegerreis,

Lassiter, David. Forestry Definitions. Mississippi Forestry Association

Hubbard, Latt, Long, Forest Terminology for Multiple Use Management

LaVergne, TN USA
02 January 2010
210730LV00005B